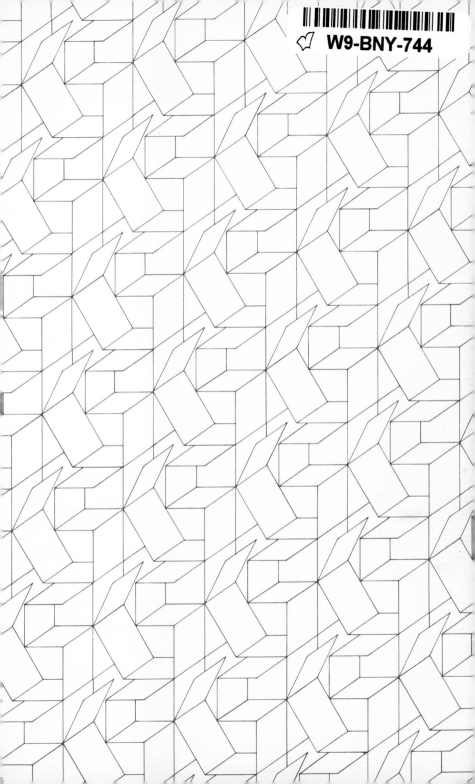

KARL SHAPIRO

PERSON, PLACE AND THING

V-LETTER AND OTHER POEMS

ESSAY ON RIME

TRIAL OF A POET

POEMS 1940-1953

BEYOND CRITICISM

POEMS OF A JEW

IN DEFENCE OF IGNORANCE

THE BOURGEOIS POET

SELECTED POEMS

TO ABOLISH CHILDREN

WHITE-HAIRED LOVER

WHITE-HAIRED LOVER

KARL SHAPIRO

WHITE-HAIRED LOVER

RANDOM HOUSE   NEW YORK

811
S

Some of these poems have appeared in EVERGREEN REVIEW, THE NEW YORKER,
NORTHWEST REVIEW, POETRY, TRI QUARTERLY, SATURDAY EVENING POST,
STEPPENWOLF, and OMNIBUS CHICAGOLAND.

Library of Congress Catalog Card Number: 68-31733

Manufactured in the United States of America by The Book Press, Inc.,
Brattleboro, Vermont
Designed by Richard-Gabriel Rummonds
Type set by The Typographic Service Company, New York

for TERI

My glass shall not persuade me I am old

CONTENTS

I   THERE WAS THAT ROMAN POET   3

II   YOU PLAYED CHOPIN   4

III   I SWORE TO STAB THE SONNET   5

IV   HOW BEAUTIFULLY YOU CLOTHE YOUR BODY   6

V   HE LOVES THE CHASE   7

VI   THE DARK EXCITING DAYS   8

VII THERE IS GRAY IN MY EYEBROWS   9

VIII HOW DO I LOVE YOU?   10

IX   LOVE, IT IS TIME   11

X   I DO NOT WANT TO RECOGNIZE YOUR FACE   12

XI   IF I SHOULD DIE   13

XII ROSES, POETRY   14

XIII YOU LAY ABOVE ME   15

XIV O MY BELOVED   16

XV   I AM THE CLOWN   17

XVI IT'S MORNING   18

XVII HOW DO YOU WALK?   19

XVIII IN ST. LOUIS IN A HUNDRED AND FOUR DEGREES   21

XIX IT'S GETTING READY TO STORM   22

XX   THE SAD THING IS   23

XXI AUBADE   24

XXII BALLADE   27

XXIII NOW CHRIST IS RISEN   29

XXIV WORDS FOR A WALL-PAINTING   30

XXV AFTER THE STORM   31

XXVI YOU, LYING WITH YOUR BACK TO ME   32

XXVII REEKING WITH LOVE   33

XXVIII JULY THE FOURTH   34

XXIX EPITHALAMIUM, THE SECOND TIME AROUND   35

WHITE-HAIRED LOVER

There was that Roman poet who fell in love at fifty-odd.

My God, *Venus*, goddess of love, he cried,

Venus, for Christsake, for the love of God,

Don't do that to me!

Don't let me fall in love, a man of my age.

I beg you on my knobby knees, lay off.

Basta! I've had enough — not only that,

NON SUM QUALIS ERAM, Jesus Christ!

How do you know I can get it up!

The laughter of the goddess cool as hell

Pinged like a Cellini shell.

Priceless, she said, showing her teeth, clacking her

    castanets, stomping her feet.

And what has age to do with that, Quintus, she said,

And put that in your Classical Dictionary . . .

And went her way in a wild odor of roses and garlic.

II   You played Chopin at ten at my request,
Ten in the morning while I opened beer,
Myself a somewhat uninvited guest,
Yourself lost in the melody, lost in fear.
The heavy nocturne like old damask hung
In the half-empty house while your young child
Wandered half-lost between us and among
Tables and chairs . . . myself silent and wild,
Yourself proud and resentful. Then you said
Read one of your poems, and brought the book.
Wasn't it Baudelaire's *Giantess* I read
That I'd translated on a troopship? Look,
Eleven months have passed and the birds sing
Since that strange morning that changed everything.

III I swore to stab the sonnet with my pen,
Squash the black widow in a grandstand play
By gunning down the sonnet form — and then
I heard you quote my schoolboy love Millay.
I went to find out what she used to say
About her tribulations and her men
And loved her poetry though I now am gray
And found out love of love poems once again.
Now I'm the one that's stabbed — son of a bitch!
With my own poisoned ballpoint pen of love
And write in *sonnet* form to make my *pitch*,
Words I no longer know the meaning of.
If I could write one honest sentence now
I'd say I love you but I don't know how.

IV How beautifully you clothe your body
    As if to say, undress me if you can
    And find how beautiful I really am.
    Only a beauty dares to wear a wig
    But I can cradle you and you are big
    (Minus the worship of the insincere)
    Or worship you without becoming slave
    Or post-post-adolescent Indian-brave.
    You dress burnt-orange, square-shape cotton, silk,
    Nylon and Turner, Veronese, glass,
    High-breasted with a Zeuxian-Keatsean ass,
    Alice-in-Wonderland 16—twice 16—
    As if age entered in, although it does,
    Making me love you mostly in your clothes.

V He loves the chase—that's what your sister said,
   Explaining me both to herself and you,
   And now her question occupies my head:
   What if the diagnosis should be true?
   Say it *is* true, and would that matter much,
   Would it invalidate my love to be
   Near you, about you, close enough to touch:
   What if the chase is only poetry?
   If poetry can be *only*, then I lie,
   Then it's your anger and your sadness that
   I fatten on like some neurotic guy
   Turned on by pride or drunkenness or fat.
   Okay, I love the chase, but that's not all,
   I love the catch—body and clothes and soul.

VI   There are also the dark exciting days of
The dark night of the soul
The sound of the phone like a pistol shot
And the mailman like a dangerous friend
And the master bedroom like a room redone
    in a cool museum and cordonned off
    with a silky thick and python rope
    and the great bed like a grave.
So may there be a name like the prayer OM
Name that strikes like a match in a black cave.

VII There is gray in my eyebrows, white all over my head,
Death kissing my eyes like a homosexual.
I have a fat belly from my own poetry.
Give me your full beautiful hands with freckles
My name in your voice like an arpeggio in a minor key
Your eyes glazed like those of a Mexican woman
And I am the Mexican movie general
With bandoliers of words in the dust in the eyes of cameras.

VIII How do I love you? I don't even know
Now we're cut off again like a bad phone
(Faulty communications are my middle name).
Everything is the same and not the same,
You are still here but also you are gone
And soon I shall be far away also.
How does it matter that I wish you well,
That no one weaken your resolve to go?
How do I love you? Is it just a game
To love your sadness and possess your name?
And now you have no reason to be sad
Do I lose the little of you that I had?
And if I've lost you who is there to blame?
(Faulty communications are my middle name).

IX   Love, it is time I memorized your phone
Number and made it part of what I keep
Not in a black book but in living bone
Of fingertips that dial you in my sleep.
Time that the Roman wires of my heart
Lead all to you like artery or vein
Or tourist roadmap or a fever chart,
Since you are central now to my love's brain.
Teri, I have your number in my blood,
Your name is red and racing in my pulse
And all my nerves are ringing as they should
Through the night's black and sweet umbilicus
Connecting our two lives with strings of words
That you send back this spring like flights of birds.

X   I do not want to recognize your face
In that dead portrait where you stand so tall
And ritualistic in your marriage lace;
I cannot see you in that world at all.
Now we're in love although the hour is late
And I'm the one that's straining toward your life
Inevitably as by some kind of fate
That makes you mine, my mistress or my wife,
Muse, idol of worship, woman-child,
Mother or friend or object of my lust.
Only you make me truly reconciled
To all that joy that had become my ghost;
So from your newfound sleep I resurrect
This love, both yours supine, and mine erect.

XI "If I should die think only this of me"
I love you more than my mosaic heart
Made out of all the loves I've ever known
And finally come full circle in your own.
No, I don't want you as a work of art
Or stained-glass of my private history,
My Ourobourous, Jesus on his Tree
Or Moses' tablets which he smashed to bits
Because the children of Israel were lewd!
If you're my idol then I'll call it quits.
I want you housewife, eveninggown and nude,
Divorcee, mother of your daughters, mine,
With all your past that you're the total of,
Plus my corrupt antiquity which you love.

XII   "Roses, poetry, and a sensual voice.
      Oh, Christ! What if that's all he wants to give."
      Yes, for how long can love expect to live
      On flowers and poems, such therapeutic toys
      As tears and music, phonecalls in the dark,
      The slant of danger in the rented room —
      For one can have and hold no matter whom,
      And any street will do on which to park.
      What too if all he has to give is peace,
      Sympathy, admiration, tender awe,
      All those *abstractions!* Wells from which to draw
      Sweet dreams or happy laughter or heart's ease.
      But all in all, if these have not sufficed,
      You have a right to agonize: "Oh, Christ!"

XIII   You lay above me on that beautiful day,
       Your dark eyes made more dark with tiny wings
       You drew to prick my kisses with beestings.
       Your russet hair in heavy brushstrokes lay
       Against the pastel of the Nebraska sky
       And all around the stippled poplar trees
       Framed you like an unpainted masterpiece.
       Some birds spoke out and airplanes coming over,
       And now and then a farmer peered our way
       Where we were stretched out on the new green grass
       On a green blanket, to see a white-haired lover
       And a wine-colored, flower-printed creature,
       As mythologically dark and dazzling as
       The sun that forces frozen earth to nature.

XIV O my beloved and the days go by
And we can't tell which day or week or why
Because what does it matter when I have
The long-eyed Renoir *enfant* that you gave,
Knowing it has your sweet ambiguous eyes
Which now I kiss, your hands that tantalize,
Your breasts that open to me and your thighs,
Your arms that lift up music from the keys,
Your shadowy voice with all its harmonies,
The words you write and those we read together,
The wine you take into your perfect lips
From mine, your tongue made musky by those grapes,
Your look of parting like a darkening sky,
Your wave as sovereign as a peacock feather.

XV   I am the clown that laughs and cries into your life
Knocking you down and picking you up,
And you are the last woman in the laughing arena of my life.
In the darkened garden of upturned faces
I fall in terror from the absurd highwire
Into the love-net of your spangled arms,
And when you wipe the greasepaint of my tears
And when you rearrange my smile
With tears and laughter in the front seat of a car
Aimlessly floating through obscure back streets and over
    the humpback country roads
Which send up dust clouds of applause into the rawsilk
    scarves of sky,
We kiss to the patriotic ridiculous roll of drums
And fall into the spaceless spaces of each other.

XVI It's morning and I meet your morning mind
Like flakking open the venetian blind
Or better yet those signal lights at sea
On darkened battleships that dangerously
Send absolute messages only each to each.
Today you say I cannot take that beach.
Tonight you'll say we'll try. Ah but the war
Is over, and we lie on chosen shore,
Some St. Tropez where morning is our night
And there are no more enemies to fight
Except love's own sweet battle. Lie in my arms
Naked and open to ten thousand storms
I dream of rocketing into your loins
And deep into your sea where no sun shines.

XVII How do you walk? You walk into my arms,
Into my kiss, into the eye of my life's storm.
You walk (all similies are silly in my love for you)
You walk as if you were carrying the Taj Mahal.
Your neck is like a Watusi woman towering above the grasses
    of your tigerish clothes,
Your tribal shoulders where my fingers close and feed and
    my lips graze like sheep-crazed shepherds.
You walk in anger and in glorious pride as if you had lost a
    brilliant naval battle,
Your cut smile belies your perspicuous eyes,
Your earrings tremble and your breasts rise like waves
    of liquid in your coming toward me.
Your hips powerful and civilized make idiots of willow
    trees plying the prairie winds,
You carry your hard-soft hands as if they were not yours
    but mine.
Is it your long proud legs that carry you into my vision
    like rhyme?
You walk as if you were carrying a love-child,
You walk as if you were marrying me,

And your sensitive head turns slightly side to side

As not to see the lovely commotion of your passing,

Where you have come from but only where you are going.

Where are you going? You are going into your beauty

And it is I who am opening all the doors as you pass

From room to room of your life till you walk to my grave.

XVIII In St. Louis in a hundred and four degrees,
I bought an aquamarine of purest cut,
Then drove eight hundred miles just like a breeze
To place it on your finger, "on my knees"
Engaging you, I guess—I don't know what—
To be my wife, to make your hand my hand.
That afternoon you shed your wedding band
You little knew, nor I, how deeply wed
We were to one another, ring or no ring,
How truly oned and all those vows all said
That lovers trade to bind up everything.
Now let our marriage steadily increase
Till I have banded you and signed our lease
And kissed you for the justice of the peace.

XIX It's getting ready to storm, you're on your way
Back from the garden of your own first house,
Back to my life and our emerging vows,
Driving as if you were driving very May
Into my love-burst heart — and may no harm
Befall you or your pretty ones, and may
Engulfing June sweep all our fears away
And drive us free of our divorces' storm.
How far? Far into the future, very far,
Far into Europe where our pasts entwine,
And farther still into these present hours
When you drive toward me in your flowery car
To say *I'm back*, which means that you are mine,
Back from your house, where you were planting flowers.

XX The sad thing is about our mutual friend
She didn't bless our happiness or seem
To give a damn about its rightful end
Unlike the tender rabbi of your dream
Who blessed the child in us and let us play
The child out in your wish-fulfilling sleep.
His was a gentle warning on our way,
Hers was a threat, the sad desire to keep
Unhappiness the norm of all love-life.
That afternoon we drank to her return
We all three laughed but yet had still to learn
Her symbol of the hand struck by a knife.
It's our first loss and though we share her pain
This loss may be our most important gain.

AUBADE

Et c'est la fin pour quoy sommes ensemble.

XXI What dawn is it?
The morning star stands at the end of your street as
   you watch me turn to laugh a kind of goodbye, with
   love-crazed head like a white satyr moving through
   wet bushes.
The morning star bursts in my eye like a hemorrhage as
   I enter my car in a dream surrounded by your
   heavenly-earthly smell.
The steering wheel is sticky with dew,
The golf course is empty, husbands stir in their sleep
   desiring, and though no cocks crow in suburbia, the
   birds are making a hell of a racket.
Into the newspaper dawn as sweet as your arms that hold
   the old new world, dawn of green lights that smear the
   empty streets with come and go.
It is always dawn when I say goodnight to you,
Dawn of wrecked hair and devastated beds,
Dawn when protective blackness turns to blue and lovers
   drive sunward with peripheral vision.
—To improvise a little on Villon,
Dawn is the end for which we are together.

My house of loaded ashtrays and unwashed glasses, tulip
     petals and columbine that spill on the table and
     splash on the floor,
My house full of your dawns,
My house where your absence is presence,
My slum that loves you, my bedroom of dustmice and cobwebs,
     of local paintings and eclectic posters, my bedroom
     of rust neckties and divorced mattresses, and of
     two of your postcards, *Pierrot with Flowers* and
     Young Girl with Cat,
My bed where you have thrown your body down like a
     king's ransom or a boa constrictor.
But I forgot to say: May passed away last night,
May died in her sleep.
That May that blessed and kept our love in fields and
     motels.
I erect a priapic statue to that May for lovers to kiss
     as long as I'm in print, and polish as smooth as the
     Pope's toe.
This morning came June of spirea and platitudes,
This morning came June discreetly dressed in gray,

June of terrific promises and lawsuits.

And where are the poems that got lost in the shuffle
of spring?

Where is the poem about the eleventh of March, when we
raised the battleflag of dawn?

Where is the poem about the coral necklace that whipped
your naked breasts in leaps of love?

The poem concerning the ancient lover we followed through
your beautiful sleeping head?

The fire-fountain of your earthquake thighs and your
electric mouth?

Where is the poem about the little one who says my name
and watches us almost kissing in the sun?

The vellum stretchmarks on your learned belly,

Your rosy-fingered nightgown of nylon and popcorn,

Your razor that caresses your calves like my hands?

Where are the poems that are already obsolete, leaves
of last month, a very historical month?

Maybe I'll write them, maybe I won't, no matter,

And this is the end for which we are together.

Et c'est la fin pour quoy sommes ensemble.

BALLADE

XXII

Here ends this cycle of my poems for you
Since we have passed from poetry into life,
You give me everything that love can do,
I think you say you want to be my wife,
Yet some suspicion pricks me like a knife
As if some guilty party, you or I,
Shadows our love with doubt and disbelief
That you will not be with me till I die.

Or bastard that I am and poet and Jew
As you grow quiet and strong I cause you grief,
Fighting what I desire, the group of two,
And thieve your beauty like a sickly thief,
Possessing you in phantasy — in brief
Betraying all this joy for poetry,
So terrified our love will not be safe,
That you will not be with me till I die.

My heart knows none of this is really true,
The fear, the guilt, the business of the grave.
What haven't you given, what haven't you made new
And strong and beautiful in this twilight cave?
You give me everything that love can crave,
You give me everything that love can try,
You even liberate me as love's slave:
"That you will not be with me till I die."

Dear love, our love is only what we gave
And what awaits, whether we laugh or cry;
God strike me if I question what we have
And that you'll not be with me till I die.

XXIII   Now Christ is risen in his freudian hat
And Nature's gussied up with palms of gilt
And I myself have risen, and all that,
I stand in Paradise and will not wilt,
And praise your atheism to the skies.
I drive my Jesus homeward to the hilt
And nail you to the cross until He dies.
And you, belov'd Teresa of my soul,
Carry me to the brink with iron cries,
Mother my masterpiece until I'm whole
And sail me into Palestinian bliss
While I lie glowing like a fading coal.
Scholar: no need of your analysis:
Love's the life-cycle of a lifer's kiss.

XXIV   On this wall like child I write I love you
Public and private graffiti of my heart,
Sun of your love lays bare these simple lines
Like a Pompeiian bedroom lit with gold
And black Vesuvian plume. As pink as stone
Your hand uncovers me. Round as a Bay
Your form encircles my form night and day,
And deep as Mare Nostrum with sweet salt
Washes whole centuries of sleep away.
This is the time of finding hour by hour
The streets and alleys of our ecstasy.
This is the place to sign my syllables
Of deep relief on tiny tiles of sound,
And may my words still stand when the wall falls.
This is a poem to write upon your wall,
My wall, our wall, to meet us in the eye
In the dawnlight of Chicago furry-gray
When garbage truck groans in the alley-way,
Sparrows chitter and pigeons make their moan.
On this wall like child I write I love you
I write I love you in our private moan.
I paint I love you Teri and sign Karl.

AFTER THE STORM

XXV   After the storm the trees lift up their hands
Unmindful of the lumber that has crashed
Below and crushed the flora of its lands.
The lands are littered and the air is washed.

We pick the pieces up after the storm,
Wonder at wood we never knew was there
And wonder at the whirlwind of the worm
That tore the world in two and washed the air.

The diamond morning walks on broken glass,
Or is it tears we see through in our kiss
After the wreckage of the night that has
Unblinded us and stripped the ponderous trees.

I love you and I fall upon my knees
And gather you like heavens of sweet grass.

XXVI   You, lying with your back to me,
        Lie there in majesty, and when you wake,
        Turn the black sunlight of your eyes my way,
        And I will rise and take you in my arms.
        Sleep well and welcome me.

XXVII   Reeking with love we lay upon our bed
Your hand upon my heart, my hand upon
Your hand, white upon white on red,
Our bodies nesting deeply, having fed.

And so we sank to almost dreamless sleep,
Your cooling bosom pressed into my back,
Until your hand gave an escapeful leap,
As pigeons bite each other in the neck

Prior to pigeoning, and your hand took wing
And plummeted below to try to find
The single snake awake and burgeoning
To make of heart and hand a single mind.

Turning sweet nighttime into sweeter day
Your fingers closed around my beast of prey.

XXVIII

July the Fourth, bombs bursting in air
Over the golf course and your patio;
I am reduced to cinders by your glare,
While outside populations *ah!* and *oh!*

"I can't even remember what that fight
Was all about. You drove around with him
Under the bloom of rockets' bursting light—
Income tax, I think, or something grim."

The wiles of lofty Liberty are droll,
Sweet brazen Liberty that makes our laws
And sets up freedom's rosy, golden pole.
Her hand of fire is first to quench the cause:

Fierce Liberty that lights us on our way,
March us with torches to our wedding day!

XXIX   Marriage, killer of many a love, is dead,

Hymen, O Hymenaee,

But we today remarry in the name of love,

Hymen, Hymenaee O,

And now I come to shake you from your sleep

And come to do your ancient ritual wrong.

Greatest of all the gods (Catullus said,

Considering all the Romans that you wed

With torchlight and with bridal song)

Classical god, accompany us to court

To shine your flame upon our tiny company;

I promise you the ceremony is short;

Hymen, O Hymenaee, witness our way.

I woke my love with kisses on her skin,

Hymen, O Hymenaee,

"Darling, wake up, this is our second-wedding day!"

Hymen, Hymenaee O,

I woke my love with kisses on her hair,

I woke my love with kisses on her feet,

Her hands, her lips, her nipples, and her flank.

"The beauty parlor, the barber shop, the bank!

Hurry, get dressed, we've got to meet

The judge in just two hours without fail . . ."
I woke my love, who arched her body in her usual way,
Bent like a bow. "Darling, I'll get the mail,
You make the coffee." Smiling, there she lay.

The judge's robe is silk of somber black,
Hymen, O Hymenaee,
It's strange to marry underneath the American flag,
Hymen, Hymenaee O.
The flag is silky red and white and blue,
The lipstick of my love is Barely Pink,
Her dress and coat are silken subtle white,
I, like the judge, am dressed in shades of night,
My jacket is raw silk, I think;
Three friends stand by to legalize our vows
And all is kissed and signed, and all is signed and sealed;
Delicious lunch, we rush back to our house
Which is our bed, our workshop, and our shield.

No Christ was born today and no Rome fell,
Hymen, O Hymenaee,
No Loch Ness monster showed her coils, no Ultimate weapon,
Hymen, Hymenaee O,

Incinerated Wall Street or Dubuque,
No Lisbon leapt into the bottomless bay.
"Darling, do something for me, why not play
That Chopin nocturne in the light of day,
The one that's posthumous, you say."
—The moon edges its body through the clouds
Like silver boiling over on a sky of slate
Or like Vesuvius when its golden roads
Enclosed a city in a golden gate.

Such is the ring she wears upon her hand,
Hymen, O Hymenaee,
Such is the lengthy journey that I had her go,
Hymen, Hymenaee O,
Such is the balance of this love we bear
Of weights and pleasures of our psyches' woe;
Wide is the ring and what we understand
Deeper and wider than this wildest land
On which we travel to and fro
Perennially laughing in this weeping womb
Of war, technology, calendars and other dangerous play.
Souviens-toi, Hymen O Hymenaee,
And thanks for rising on our wedding day.

ABOUT THE AUTHOR

Karl Shapiro was born in Baltimore, Maryland, and attended the University of Virginia and Johns Hopkins University. In 1946 he was appointed Consultant in Poetry at the Library of Congress, and then, in 1947, he joined the faculty of Johns Hopkins University, where he taught writing courses. From 1950 to 1956 he was editor of POETRY: A MAGAZINE OF VERSE. He was professor of English and editor of THE PRAIRIE SCHOONER at the University of Nebraska from 1956 to 1966 and professor of English at the Chicago Circle Campus of the University of Illinois from 1966 to 1968. He is now professor of English at the University of California at Davis. He is a member of the National Institute of Arts and Letters. His second volume of verse, V-LETTER AND OTHER POEMS, was awarded the Pulitzer Prize in 1945.